I'm Sorry,
I Can't Qui

Jonathan Lynn's London theatre debut was as Motel the Tailor in the original West End cast of *Fiddler on the Roof*. His London directing credits include *The Glass Menagerie*, *Songbook* (Best Musical – Olivier Award and Evening Standard Award), *Anna Christie* (RSC, Stratford and Donmar), *The Unvarnished Truth*, *Loot*, Eric Idle's *Pass the Butler*, *Arms and the Man*, *Tonight at Eight-Thirty*, David Wood's *The Plotters of Cabbage Patch Corner* and *The Gingerbread Man* (twice, at the Old Vic). At the National Theatre: Feydeau's *A Little Hotel on the Side* translated by John Mortimer, *Jacobowsky and the Colonel* and *Three Men on a Horse* (Olivier Award, Best Comedy). As Artistic Director of the Cambridge Theatre Company (1977–81) he directed nineteen productions, including *Macbeth* and *The Relapse*, and produced twenty others. Nine of these shows transferred to London.

He has directed ten feature films, notably *My Cousin Vinny* and *The Whole Nine Yards*, and written three (*Clue*, *Nuns on the Run* and *The Internecine Project*). His many TV performances include the memorable plays *Barmitzvah Boy*, *The Knowledge* and *Outside Edge*. He has written dozens of episodes of TV comedy series and is best known for the multi-award winning *Yes Minister* and *Yes Prime Minister*, created and written with Antony Jay. He co-wrote and directed the stage play *Yes Prime Minister* and wrote the best-selling books *The Complete Yes Minister* and *The Complete Yes Prime Minister,* still in print after more than thirty years. He wrote and directed the play *The Patriotic Traitor.* His books include the novels *Mayday* and *Samaritans*, and *Comedy Rules*, a sort of memoir.

also by Jonathan Lynn from Faber

for the stage

YES PRIME MINISTER
(*with Antony Jay*)

THE PATRIOTIC TRAITOR

prose

COMEDY RULES

JONATHAN LYNN

I'm Sorry, Prime Minister, I Can't Quite Remember . . .

The Final Chapter

faber

First published in 2023
by Faber and Faber Limited
The Bindery, 51 Hatton Garden
London, EC1N 8HN

Typeset by Brighton Gray
Printed and bound in the UK by CPI Group (Ltd), Croydon CR0 4YY

A CIP record for this book
is available from the British Library

978-0-571-38807-3

Printed and bound in the UK on FSC® certified paper in line with our continuing
commitment to ethical business practices, sustainability and the environment.
For further information see faber.co.uk/environmental-policy

2 4 6 8 10 9 7 5 3 1

I'm Sorry, Prime Minister, I Can't Quite Remember . . . was first performed at the Barn Theatre, Cirencester, on 22 September 2023.

Jim Hacker Jonathan Lynn
Sir Humphrey Appleby Clive Francis
Sophie Michaela Bennison
Sir David Knell Christopher Bianchi

Director Jonathan Lynn
Set and Costume Designer Lee Newby
Sound Consultant Sam Glossop
Lighting Designer Adam Foley

The play is based on the characters developed for
Yes Minister and *Yes Prime Minister*
by Antony Jay and Jonathan Lynn,
and is dedicated to the memory of Antony Jay

Characters

Jim Hacker

Sophie

Sir David Knell

Sir Humphrey Appleby

Setting

The living room of the Master's Lodge
at Hacker College, Oxford.

I'M SORRY, PRIME MINISTER, I CAN'T QUITE REMEMBER . . .

Act One

The living room of the Master's Lodge at Hacker College, Oxford. The room is modern, because the college was built about fifteen years ago. It is open plan. There is a kitchen area (perhaps partly offstage) and doors/exits to a study/library and the hall.

It was once comfortably furnished but is now a scruffy, untidy mess. Big, overflowing packing boxes, papers strewn everywhere, bookshelves untidy. A half-eaten sandwich and a pizza box on a messy dining table.

There are windows, French or otherwise, looking out onto an wintry garden – bare trees. It is a sunny morning.

Jim, an old man who is largely but untidily dressed, buttons in the wrong buttonholes on his cardigan and wearing no shoes or socks, sits in a comfy chair. A Zimmer frame stands nearby.

He is talking to Sophie, an attractive Black woman in her early thirties.

Jim Have you got a CV?

Sophie Yes.

She hands it to him. He doesn't look at it.

Jim What are you, a nurse? Social worker?

Sophie Neither. Sorry.

Jim Have you any references?

Sophie Here.

She hands some letters to him. He looks at them hopelessly.

Jim Um, I haven't got my glasses. Tell me about yourself.

Sophie Nothing much to tell really.

Jim Have you done this kind of work before?

Sophie I cared for my mum and my dad. They both had dementia. So, yes.

Jim I don't have dementia. Or Alzheimer's.

Sophie (*encouraging*) That's good.

Jim I have lower back pain. Arthritis in my knees. Bad hip. Oh, and gout. Apart from that I'm completely fine.

Sophie That's nice.

Jim Oh – and congestive heart failure, which makes me a bit breathless sometimes. It's hard to . . . do things.

Sophie I understand. That's why you need me.

Jim Yes. (*Cautious.*) Or someone like you.

Sophie I see.

Jim I need help getting up, dressing, you know, putting on my shoes and socks, having a shower, that sort of thing . . . just helping, really.

Sophie All day?

Jim Well, morning and bedtime. And sometimes during the day.

Sophie No problem.

Jim I think I'm in pretty good shape for someone of my age.

Sophie How old are you?

Jim Over eighty. What do you charge?

Sophie Twelve quid an hour.

Jim Isn't that a bit steep?

Sophie It's very little. An agency would charge you twenty.

Jim But austerity and all that . . .

Sophie I know all about austerity, thank you?

Jim You understand economics?

Sophie I experience economics. I have trouble making ends meet.

Jim Perhaps you need to economise a little.

Sophie Poor people can't afford to economise.

Jim I'm glad you didn't say you understand economics because nobody does really. (*Indicates ring finger.*) I see you're married. What does your husband do?

Sophie I haven't got a husband.

Jim Oh. Divorced?

Sophie I've got a wife.

Jim Ah. How very . . . modern of you. So, why do you want to be a carer?

Sophie I don't. A carer takes care of a family member for free, helps them shower, dress, eat. I would be what's called a care *worker.*

Jim I see. Like sex worker?

Sophie (*firm*) No, nothing like.

Jim I just meant adding the word 'worker' sort of turns it into a job.

Sophie It's a job whatever word you add. I thought you'd like to know the correct terminology as you're the head of an academic institution.

Jim I just was asking why you want to do it.

Sophie I like caring for people. I'm good at it.

Jim But no qualifications of any sort?

Sophie I didn't say that. I said I'm not a nurse or a social worker.

Jim So what do you have? GCSEs?

Sophie Yes. And a degree.

Jim Oh. Where from?

Sophie Oxford.

Jim Oxford? *Really?* Which college?

Sophie This college. I was in your second year's intake.

Jim A degree from Hacker College! Wonderful! Did you love it here?

Sophie I hated it.

Jim (*surprised*) Why?

Sophie All the entitled public-school kids. I was very uncomfortable, I didn't belong, I couldn't breathe.

Jim That's changing. They're not all from public schools now. And there are lots of girls here now.

Sophie Yes, some women too.

Jim Oh yes, women, not girls, sorry. I can say women?

Sophie You can say women. There was nobody else here from a council estate in Tottenham.

Jim What a pity you didn't enjoy it here. What did you read?

Sophie English.

Jim That explains why you're just a carer. Care worker. Why you can't get a decent job . . .

Sophie If that's your opinion of this job, I don't think I want it.

She stands up.

Jim No. Wait a minute. Sorry . . . I just meant, if you'd done computer studies, something useful, technological, that equips you for the modern world . . .

Sophie Studying English is *not* useful?

Jim No, no I just meant something with career prospects. What can you do with an English degree other than become a teacher? (*Disparaging.*) Or an academic.

Sophie And as master of a college you don't think there's any point in being an academic?

Jim That's not what I meant either.

Sophie That's why I hated it here. Education for its own sake isn't valued any more. It's all about jobs and targets, according to you lot.

Jim My lot?

Sophie Politicians. It doesn't seem to make much difference which party's in power.

Jim I agree. That's why I sit on the cross benches now. And believe me, I'm sometimes pretty cross. (*Chuckles at his own joke.*) So, um, why do you want this job? Is it because I'm famous?

Sophie (*amused*) Certainly not.

Jim I used to be prime minister, you know.

Sophie I know. You were an important man once.

Jim (*offended*) Still am! Master of an Oxford college named after me.

Sophie We've met before, you know.

Jim Have we? I'm so sorry, I don't remember.

Sophie I wouldn't expect you to. You were the Master while I was here. I came to your freshers' sherry party.

Jim How did you hear I needed someone?

Sophie Jeff said you needed a bit of help.

Jim Jeff?

Sophie One of the porters. You don't know them by name?

Jim I'm not good at names any more.

She stands up and looks around.

Sophie This place is a bit – (*She pulls a face.*) Do you have a cleaner?

Jim She hasn't been in. I've had the same one for four years, I paid her above the going rate, then suddenly she phones and says she can't come in because her husband's just been diagnosed with cancer. (*Bitter.*) That's how she repays me.

Sophie Poor thing.

Jim But what about me? Look at the mess here!

Sophie Apart from a good cleaning, what you need is a filing system.

Jim Organising stuff was never my forte.

Sophie How did you manage as prime minister then?

Jim Oh, the civil servants do all that.

Sophie (*sits*) May I ask you a personal question?

Jim (*grand*) You'll find everything you need to know about me in *Who's Who*.

Sophie Not this. Are you incontinent?

Jim (*embarrassed*) Incontinent? What a question!

Sophie If you are, it's nothing to be ashamed of, it comes to most of us in the end. But I'd need to know. (*She waits.*) It's just between us.

Jim I'm not! I do – er – I occasionally have an accident, but . . .

Sophie That's no problem.

Jim changes the subject.

Jim What did you do before you started taking care of your parents?

Sophie Teacher training.

Jim Were you sorry to give it up?

Sophie Yes. But I'd just done a dissertation on *Hamlet*.

Jim Oh yes?

Sophie It was on Renunciation and Acceptance. Hamlet says, 'The readiness is all.' I found that very helpful.

Jim Readiness for what?

Sophie Hamlet's talking about death. He says the point is not when a man will die, but that he is ready.

Jim Hmm. So, you gave up your career?

Sophie No choice. Somebody had to take care of my parents. My brother couldn't, or wouldn't. No real social care – you know, austerity. It was really hard, but I loved them.

Jim I see.

Sophie Now they're gone, I'm sort of rethinking while I decide what I want to do with my life.

Jim You don't want to be a carer, surely?

Sophie looks at him for a moment.

Sophie You know . . . I'm really not sure this is a good idea.

Jim What isn't?

Sophie Looking after you. I'm afraid we mightn't get along.

Jim No, wait. Don't get me wrong, I really like to be around intelligent young people with their lives before them, who think I'm wise and treat me with respect.

Sophie (*tries to repress a smile*) I see.

Jim That's why I took the job as master of a college. Not just that, I have a voice in the university, I'm in the House of Lords, I have this lovely permanent home. Everything's hunky-dory. I just need a bit of help.

Sophie looks at him, appraises him.

Sophie So. Would you like me to do this?

Jim Er – yes.

Sophie How would you feel about a try-out period?

Jim Good idea. I can try you out.

Sophie And I can try *you* out.

Jim Oh – yes. Right. Let's start. So – find my glasses. And put on my shoes and socks.

Sophie Please.

Jim What?

Sophie Please.

Jim I don't think I – ?

Sophie This is a try-out, remember?

Jim What are you saying?

Sophie Do you want me to respect you?

Jim Of course. I just said so.

Sophie Then respect me.

Jim Do you realise who I am? I had my finger on the nuclear button.

Sophie Thank God you haven't now.

She offers him his glasses, which were close by. He takes the glasses, puts them on, then shoves them up on to his forehead. She starts putting on one of his socks which are also nearby, abandoned on the floor.

Lift up your foot.

Jim Please.

Sophie (*amused*) This is for you, not me. I frankly don't care if you've got your socks on or not. Now, lift up your foot, please.

The phone rings.

Sophie Shall I get it?

Jim Yes.

She doesn't move.

(*Gritted teeth.*) Please!

She answers it.

Sophie Master's residence . . . Hi, Jeff . . . Okay, I think, but who knows? . . . I see. Has he an appointment? . . . Okay.

She rings off.

Jim Has who an appointment?

Sophie The Visitor. He's at the Porter's Lodge, on his way over.

Jim Who? What visitor?

Sophie Dunno. Jeff just said 'The Visitor'.

Jim But who is it?

Sophie (*cheerful*) Maybe it's like Goldberg or McCann in *The Birthday Party*.

Jim Whose birthday party?

Sophie Or the Mysterious Stranger in *The Lady from the Sea*.

Jim What are you talking about?

Sophie Ibsen. *The Lady from the Sea*. Surely you've heard of Ibsen?

Jim Yes.

Sophie Did you ever see *The Seventh Seal*?

Jim Yes of course! One of Ibsen's finest plays.

Sophie It's a film by Ingmar Bergman. There's a nameless visitor in that too. In a black cowl. With a scythe.

Jim You mean – ?

Sophie The visitor is the Grim Reaper.

Jim (*panicking*) Oh my God!

The doorbell rings.

Sophie There he is now.

She heads for the door and exits.

Jim Oh God!

He stands up and retreats, scared. Sophie returns with a tall, thin, elderly man in a dark suit and a black coat and hat. She announces him.

Sophie The Visitor.

Jim What do you want with me?

David We have a meeting. Perhaps you've forgotten what it's about.

Jim I don't forget things. I have the best memory in the Commons.

Sophie You're in the Lords.

Jim Shut up, Sophie.

David Is it still convenient?

Jim (*nervous laugh*) Depends what it is. I suppose so. Nice to meet you, anyway.

David We've met before. At High Table, several times.

Jim I meant nice to see you again.

David I understand your trying to avoid this meeting . . .

Jim Why should I try to avoid it?

David Perhaps I should remind you.

Jim Yes, do.

David May I sit down?

Jim Of course. Sorry. Have to be polite to the Grim Reaper.

David I'd rather you didn't call me that.

Jim You mean, you *are*?

David Well, only in a manner of speaking.

Jim What manner is that, exactly?

Sophie Do you want me to stay?

Jim I think you'd better.

Sophie May I take your coat?

As they sit, Sophie hangs it up and sits somewhere out of the way.

David I'm Sir David Knell, we've met at a few High Table dinners but perhaps I should remind you: I'm a judge.

Jim You mean, this is . . . Judgement Day?

David No. Not until next week.

Jim gives a frightened yelp.

Not that I'd call it that. Let me explain.

Jim I'd be most grateful.

David I'm a High Court Judge and I used to tutor law students here. Being 'The Visitor' is usually just a sinecure, as I'm sure I don't need to remind *you*, it's honorary, just for the rare event of there being a serious dispute within the college fellowship. Nothing to do, normally.

Jim Can we get to the point?

David Well, as I'm sure I don't need to remind you, this dispute isn't among the Fellows but between the college and you. They insist that it's time for you to stand down.

Jim (*deep sigh*) This college was so much more congenial in lockdown when they were all at home and the teaching was online.

David But they're back and they want you to stand down.

Jim I've told them, the answer's no.

David I'm afraid you have no choice.

Jim I don't think *they* do.

David I think you'll find . . .

Jim This could get ugly.

David As I'm sure I don't need to remind you, most college masters have a fixed term at the end of which their job is either renewed or they can resign. But they can't go past the retirement age of seventy-five. You are well past that age, and I'm afraid your time has come.

Jim Nothing in the college statutes that says I have to resign. It's my college. Named after me. It was a tribute to me.

David The college knows that, and appreciates it, but it's not actually *yours*.

Jim I raised the bulk of the money from a wealthy donor on two conditions: one, that I would be the first Master, and two, that I could stay until I chose to retire. Which I don't. It was a lifetime appointment.

David That's true, but in retrospect that arrangement is viewed as a mistake.

Jim Not by me. They can't force me out.

David I'm afraid they can. And will.

Jim Are you serious?

David As I'm sure I don't need to remind –

Jim You keep saying that – and no, you don't!

David My apologies – the final meeting is next Wednesday. But they are hoping we can settle it amicably now.

Jim You don't seem to realise, I was the prime minister! I have cards to play.

David I'm afraid the college is adamant.

Jim So am I. You may go.

David Very well. (*Stands.*) I'm so sorry to be the bearer of bad tidings. But there it is.

He leaves.

Sophie Do you have cards to play?

Jim Yes. I'm phoning Sir Bernard Woolley. Used to be my private secretary. Became Head of the Home Civil Service. He owes me.

Jim stands up. Wobbles. She gets the Zimmer frame but he waves it away. He finds an address book on his desk and leafs through it.

Can you read this number? I've lost my glasses.

Sophie They're on your head.

Jim dials.

Jim Hello? Lady Woolley . . . Jim Hacker here . . .
(*Bright and cheerful.*) Yes, Jim Hacker! . . . No I'm not dead, I'm in the House of Lords . . . Can I speak to Bernard? . . .
He's *dead*? Oh, shit! Are you serious? . . .
No, I'm sorry, of course you're serious . . . I mean, my condolences . . .
Three *years* ago? . . .
I was at the funeral? . . . Are you sure?

He turns to Sophie.

She hung up on me.

He sits, very sad.

Sophie Was that your last card?

Jim I might have one more. Less promising though.

Sophie Less promising than dead? Not *that* promising then.

Jim Ever heard of Sir Humphrey Appleby?

Sophie No.

Jim How soon forgotten! I've got his mobile number. If he's still allowed a phone.

Sophie Why wouldn't he be?

Jim He's in St Dymphna's Home for the Elderly Deranged.

He dials, listens.

It's ringing. Oh, hello, Humphrey, Jim Hacker here . . .
Yes, a voice from the past . . .
I'm fine. More to the point, how are you? . . .
Oh good. Can you come for coffee sometime in the next few days?
Yes I know it's a long way, I suppose I could give you lunch . . .

Well, there is a bit of a hurry. Urgent problem . . .
Not until then? . . .
Oh. All right. At Hacker College, Master's Lodge . . .

He hangs up.

Coming on Wednesday. Old friend. Nearly as old as me.

Sophie Is he all right?

Jim I hope so. But he *is* in a home for the elderly deranged. That's why I called him Humphrey.

Sophie Isn't that his name?

Jim Yes, but I thought I'd better mention it in case he'd forgotten it.

Blackout.

The doorbell chimes.

Lights up. Outside the window, it is snowing. The room is somewhat tidier and less messy, the half-eaten sandwich and pizza box have gone and the mass of cardboard boxes and paper has been somewhat rearranged tidily.

Sophie hurries out of the study door and opens the front door. Sir Humphrey enters. He is around the same age as Jim. His umbrella is wet.

Sophie Sir Humphrey?

Humphrey Yes.

Sophie Please come in. Lord Hacker's just had a little nap in his study. I'm getting him up, excuse me a moment.

She hurries back to the study. Sir Humphrey looks around for somewhere to put his wet umbrella.

The study door reopens and Jim emerges, helped a little by Sophie. He is now wearing shoes and socks, and a different shirt. He is slightly less untidy. He throws his arms wide for a big hug.

Jim Humphrey! Long time no see. Welcome!

As Jim goes to hug him Humphrey recoils, and firmly extends a hand to shake. They shake hands.

Humphrey Prime Minister!

Jim No, no, not any more, that's all over.

Humphrey Indeed. Ancient history.

Sophie May I take your hat and coat, Sir Humphrey?

Humphrey Thank you.

Humphrey takes them off and hands them to Sophie.

Jim Oh, this is Sophie.

Humphrey How do you do?

Sophie Fine, thanks.

Jim She's my carer.

Sophie Your what?

Jim Care worker. Very bright girl. Woman.

Sophie nods. She goes to hang up Humphrey's hat, coat and scarf.

Thanks for coming over.

Humphrey (*gloomy*) Well . . . nothing much else to do.

Jim How did you get here?

Humphrey Somebody who works at St Dymphna's very kindly drove me.

Sophie A nurse?

Humphrey As it happens, yes. Pavelcek.

Jim What?

Humphrey My driver's name is Pavelcek.

Jim Funny name.

Humphrey He's an immigrant. But very capable in spite of that.

Jim Please, sit down.

Humphrey Thank you.

They sit.

Jim Where's he from? Your nurse.

Humphrey (*loud and clear*) My. Driver. He's from Kranjska Gora.

Jim How absolutely lovely! (*Thinks.*) Where is that, exactly?

Humphrey About an hour away from Ljubljana, in the Upper Carniola region. The nearest city is Jesenice.

Jim That's Yugoslavia isn't it?

Sophie There's no such place as Yugoslavia.

Jim There certainly is! I went skiing there once.

Humphrey She's quite right, Yugoslavia is now Croatia, Serbia, Kosovo, Slovenia, Bosnia-Herzegovina and Montenegro.

Jim When did that happen?

Humphrey I'm so bad at dates now. 1995? There was a terrible civil war.

Jim Yes I remember now, quite clearly, Kranjska Gora is in Slovakia.

Sophie Slovenia.

Jim Not Slovakia?

Humphrey Slovenia. If you confuse them the people there get very upset.

Jim Not surprised. I understand tensions still run very high in the Baltics.

Humphrey Balkans.

Jim Exactly! (*Thinks.*) I actually couldn't care less about the Balkans, what were we talking about before?

Humphrey My driver. He's leaving, all his friends have gone home to the EU. Not sure how I'll manage.

Jim You haven't got a car?

Humphrey Once I had the whole of Whitehall working for me, three thousand of the best civil servants in the world. Now I need to ask a favour to be driven anywhere.

Jim 'How are the mighty fallen'!

They both nod, with sadness.

Sophie (*mischievous*) You know that line's from a gay poem?

Jim Nonsense. It's from the Bible.

Sophie Yes. David said it. 'How are the mighty fallen, in the midst of battle. O Jonathan, thou wast slain in thine high places. I am distressed blah blah blah thy love to me was wonderful, passing the love of women.'

Neither Humphrey nor Jim know how to react.

Humphrey Um – really.

Jim Sophie likes literature.

Sophie (*cheerfully*) Especially queer literature.

Humphrey Never heard the Bible described as queer literature before. (*Stands up, looks around.*) Very nice place, this. Awful mess though.

Jim Fifty years of files, no room for them all in the study. The college told me to get my own storage unit somewhere. I don't know what's in them all. Come on, Sophie, let's have some progress.

Sophie You asked me to sort out the wheat from the chaff. I'm not finding much wheat.

Jim It will all be important one day. To my biographer.

Sophie Who is that?

Jim Um – he's not been chosen yet.

Humphrey (*dry*) *So* many eager volunteers, I suppose?

Jim (*rising above it*) Plenty. The point is, filing's not my forte.

Humphrey How well I remember. But you had me.

Jim Yes. Your help was unique.

Humphrey I spotted the irony.

Jim Bernard was so efficient. Did you know he's dead, by the way?

Humphrey Yes. Years ago, I saw you at the funeral.

Jim Did you?

Humphrey sits.

Do they let you out very often?

Humphrey Let me out?

Jim Pavelthing – you said he's a nurse. Your driver.

Humphrey He is a nurse, yes.

Jim So he escorts you back there at night, does he? To St Dymphna's.

Humphrey You seem to be under some misapprehension. Let me make something clear: my faculties are fully intact and my powers of comprehension are as acute as ever they were.

Jim Sorry, I –

Humphrey I am no longer resident at St Dymphna's. Pavelcek was kind and understanding while I was there, very briefly, and he remained in touch. Nurses are badly paid, so I give him what I can afford to drive me. Helps us both.

Jim I see.

Humphrey That place was a source of considerable embarrassment to me. I should never have been there.

Jim Of course not! Why were you?

Humphrey My daughter-in-law forced me into it. Did you ever meet her?

Jim I don't think I ever met any of your family.

Humphrey Probably not. I kept them well away from politicians.

Jim Very wise. Maybe I met your wife, but I don't think she said much.

Humphrey Halda had no interest in affairs of state. She liked gardening and the WI but she was a good mother – though now I wonder about even that, in view of whom our son married.

Jim I'd heard you were in the bin – asylum – hospital. Never got round to visiting, though I meant to.

Humphrey I hardly expected you.

Jim It *is* a home for the elderly deranged. I didn't know how deranged you were. (*Cautious.*) Do you have dementia or something?

Humphrey I do not.

Jim Just a teeny-weeny little bit, maybe?

Humphrey No!

Jim No, you don't *seem* to.

Humphrey Thank you for that vote of confidence, qualified though it may be.

Jim So . . . why . . . ?

Humphrey It was all because of inheritance tax. If you give your offspring everything seven or more years before you die they don't have to pay tax on it. I gave my son and his wife everything – my savings, my house in Haslemere, my beautiful cottage in the Dordogne . . . The understanding was that if I gave it all to them in advance they would take care of all my future expenses.

Jim But they didn't?

Humphrey No. My son's wife persuaded him to sell my house immediately. She wears the trousers. I can't bear women who wear the trousers.

Sophie is wearing trousers.

I don't mean you, dear.

Jim Why did she want to sell the house?

Humphrey To pay for me at St Dymphna's. Warehousing the elderly doesn't come cheap. 'How sharper than a serpent's tooth it is to have a thankless child.'

Jim But – why a home for the elderly deranged?

Humphrey I left my car in the middle of the road and forgot to put the brake on. It slowly rolled away down the hill.

Jim Did anyone get hurt?

Humphrey Yes. Me. I went chasing after it and I tripped. Banged my head on the kerb. After that I was a little confused. Forgetful. That's how they got away with it.

Jim But . . . this is so unlike you. You were usually three steps ahead of everyone.

Humphrey Not when concussed. We had a deal that they would pay all my expenses but they said no to everything. Like dealing with the Treasury. But I think the *real* reason they tried to put me away was that I voted against Brexit.

Jim (*incredulous*) So they put you in a home for the elderly deranged?

Humphrey Please stop saying that, that's not even its name any more. That was its Victorian name.

Jim Not PC enough?

Humphrey It's considered offensive. Rightly, in my view.

Jim Sophie? Do you consider 'deranged' offensive?

Sophie Yes.

Jim You do?

Sophie Yes, in that context.

Jim How odd. 'Deranged' is just a word.

Sophie Words matter.

Jim I don't think it's offensive, merely descriptive.

Sophie If it offends, by definition it's offensive.

Humphrey Quod erat demonstrandum.

Jim (*irritated*) Where's the coffee?

Sophie In the kitchen, where d'you think?

Jim Well, go and get some!

Sophie Go and get some – what?

Jim Coffee! (*Thinks, remembers.*) Please.

Sophie (*cheerfully*) Coming up.

Sophie goes to kitchen.

Humphrey Interesting young woman.

Jim So what's the place called now? St Dymphna's Home for the Unglued?

Humphrey (*not amused*) Very droll. The full name is St Dymphna's Home for the Aging and Intellectually Challenged by Dint of Confusion and Memory Deficiency.

Jim Catchy name. Sounds like your handiwork.

Humphrey People just call it St Dymphna's. My son and his wife call it a home. Home! I love the irony.

Jim His wife sounds awful.

Humphrey She is awful. I tried to tell him before he married her but that sort of thing never goes down well.
How little one can control, it turns out, in the lives and personalities of one's children. (*Sad.*) They even sold my car. My old Jag. I loved that car – more than my son, really. It always worked, which he never did. And unlike him, it was completely reliable and never let me down. (*Sighs.*) Anyway, enough of that. I've been released.

Jim But why did your daughter-in-law – ?

Humphrey I can't explain pure evil. Church of England question really.

Jim You believe there's such a thing as pure evil?

Humphrey I do. And I sincerely hope there's a Day of Judgement coming.

Jim That's courageous of you.

Humphrey We'll find out soon enough.

Jim Not too soon I hope.

Humphrey I wouldn't mind.

Jim Really? (*Assimilates this.*) What's your daughter-in-law's name?

Humphrey Um . . . Hmm . . . Now what is it? . . . I'm sorry, I seem to have blotted it out completely, it'll come back to me in a minute, I always refer to her as the Evil Queen. You know, the wicked stepmother in Disney's *Snow White*. I took my son to the cinema when he was small.

Jim You often found time for that?

Humphrey No, just the once. I think. We – um – we never had much of a relationship.

Jim nods, with understanding. Sophie re-enters with a tray: coffee pot, mugs and biscuits. They watch her, having run out of conversation.

(*Making an effort.*) And what was *your* daughter's name again?

Jim Lucy . . . Never see her now.

Sophie With milk?

Humphrey Thank you. It's hard to be a senior politician's child. Children always come second to the career and the immense ego.

Jim Which civil servants don't have, I suppose. That's why your son turned out so well.

Humphrey No need for that.

Sophie (*pouring Jim's coffee*) My dad was a bus driver.

They look at her, not sure how to respond. Jim pretends great interest.

Jim Is that so?

Humphrey (*pretends admiration*) Good heavens!

Sophie Not much of a job. But a great dad! Insisted I had to get a good education. Made me work really hard.

Humphrey And now you're a carer. So there you are!

Sophie (*amused*) You're a patronising old bugger, aren't you?

She gives him his coffee.

Jim Sophie! You can't speak like that to Sir Humphrey . . . Even if he is a patronising old bugger.

She grins. Humphrey puts down his coffee and heads for the hat stand.

Humphrey If that's how you feel –

Jim (*hastily*) But you're not, of course. Sophie, apologise at once.

Sophie Just me?

No response.

Okay, sorry, just joking.

She gives Jim his coffee.

I'm not a carer, by the way, I'm a care worker.

Humphrey Oh, like sex worker.

Jim, drinking his coffee, explodes with laughter. Coffee everywhere.

Humphrey What's so funny?

Jim *and* **Sophie** Nothing, nothing.

Sophie (*mopping Jim*) Is it okay with you if I carry on with the filing now? Oh . . . I found this letter from a university library.

Jim What is it? I haven't got my glasses.

Sophie They're on your head. They want to know if they could have your archives.

Jim (*excited*) Really? The Bodleian?

Sophie No, it's not from Oxford.

Jim Somewhere in Cambridge?

She shakes her head.

LSE perhaps?

She indicates 'no' again.

Where, then?

Sophie A small private university in Arkansas.

Jim Arkansas?

Sophie America.

Jim That may be good. What are they offering?

Sophie To house your archives.

Jim I meant, how much are they offering?

Sophie Oh, they're not offering any money.

Jim Tell them to stuff it!

Sophie When I've sorted through it all we might find documents that a more illustrious academic body might pay for.

Humphrey You will, if he kept *my* letters and memos.

Jim gives him a look.

Our dealings with Europe could be interesting to historians. Weren't you a Remainer?

Jim Before the referendum I was in favour of Remain . . . at least, I think I was. Now I'm pro-Brexit . . . well, I think I am. No going back now, is there? But I love Europe. I love Paris in the springtime . . . Wonderful, wonderful Copenhagen. Brussels . . . sprouts . . . Roman blinds, Spanish Steps, Romanian Rhapsody, Czech . . . mate, French kisses . . . What a romantic continent! Why did it turn out to be such a screw-up?

Sophie starts work on the files.

Humphrey I fear that the government was not fully seized of the multiplicity of entanglements on this sceptr'd isle that would be involved in unwinding forty years of regulatory activity . . . a Herculean, almost Brobdingnagian task.

Jim Brobdingwhat?

Sophie (*aside to Jim*) *Gulliver's Travels*.

Humphrey Briefly . . . Although our political lords and masters may have been experts in distortion, intrigue, chicanery and subterfuge, all undeniably necessary attributes in a negotiation of considerable complexity, it was demonstrably and unarguably true that facing simple reality was beyond the capacity of the unfortunately delusional principals, those to whom the people entrusted the management of the situation who indeed had proven skills in duplicity and concealment but not, sadly, in the essential comprehension and notification of so much disagreeable information.

Jim What?

Humphrey What?

Jim I didn't quite . . .

Humphrey I thought that was pretty clear.

Jim He *is* deranged.

Humphrey I'm just explaing how they made an utter pig's breakfast out of it! But you started it.

Jim I did. Remember my big speech about how we would never let the EU force us to give up the great British sausage? I said they'd make us call it an emulsified high-fat offal tube.

What a great speech it was. (*Churchillian.*) 'We gave up our yards for metres, our pints for litres.' Pints! That was our heritage, Humphrey, really. We lost the sixpence and the shilling. (*Dabs his eye with a tissue.*) I weep for the ha'penny and the threepenny bit, the florin, the half-crown. Gone the way of all flesh.

Humphrey That speech of yours was a national disaster.

Jim That was the speech that propelled me into Number Ten.

Humphrey That's what I mean.

Jim It didn't actually represent my views, which were ambivalent about Europe. They still are.

Humphrey Ambivalence was your modus operandi, wasn't it?

Jim I may have been ambivalent sometimes but I was always decisive.

Humphrey On the contrary, you changed your mind rather a lot.

Jim Yes, but when I changed my mind I did it *decisively*!

Humphrey Decisively back and forth?

Jim Yes. I always kept an open mind.

Humphrey (*amused, to Sophie*) Open, verging on empty.

Jim What?

Humphrey Sophie – what did you think about Brexit?

Sophie I was against it. I wanted to work in Europe and Brexit slammed the door in my face. The point of the EU was to end centuries of devastating continental wars.

Jim (*with regret*) She's right. I had no idea my sausage speech would lead to this.

Humphrey You wouldn't have cared, you'd have said anything to get elected.

Jim You wanted me to. You hoped I'd be weak and ineffectual, so you'd be in charge.

Humphrey Yes.

Jim I certainly proved you wrong there.

Humphrey I'm glad you think so.

Jim If I was so weak and ineffectual, that would mean that everything that went wrong was your fault.

Humphrey It's possible to be weak and ineffectual and still obstruct good government. Look at the current lot.

Jim I agree. But I was nothing like them.

Humphrey I'm glad you think so.

Jim There was really no one else for the job.

Humphrey I'm glad you think so.

Jim Stop saying that! There wasn't.

Humphrey No, I made sure of that.

Jim And nature abhors a vacuum. Especially in government.

Humphrey If that were true, how did you become such a success?

Jim Aha! You just said I was weak and ineffectual. Now you're admitting I was a success?

Humphrey You were, until the voters got to know you.

Jim I never lost the confidence of the voters. I lost the parliamentary party. Unlike them, and you, I trusted the voters. They were lied to.

Humphrey Like you lied in your sausage speech?

Jim I didn't lie, Humphrey. I just . . . exaggerated. That speech achieved something. It made people feel connected to their government.

Humphrey A speech is not an achievement. A speech is the politicians' substitute for action. What actually happens in Parliament? Speeches, that's all! Where does *government* happen? Whitehall, that's where everything is planned and decided. Speeches are when ministers go onstage and give a performance. Parliament is just theatre.

Sophie Surely oratory makes people feel more connected to their leaders?

Humphrey Perhaps it does. But what they feel and what is real are not the same thing.

Jim That speech was about jobs in marginal constituencies, levelling up and making people outside London feel important. Why didn't you think of that?

Humphrey I did. We moved the Vehicle Licensing Centre to Swansea, corporation taxation to Southend and forced BBC TV to move to Salford. It was all extremely inconvenient and a complete waste of money and effort – but that's true of all public relations exercises. I even suggested moving the Lords, *and* the Commons, up north, to get them out of our way, they're such a pest, but you kept batting on about the architectural heritage of the Palace of Westminster. Now that rat-infested place is falling down.

Sophie Is it rat-infested?

Jim Yes. Literally.

Humphrey And figuratively.

Sophie is intrigued.

Sophie Did you always speak so frankly to each other?

Jim *He* didn't. He was always plotting, conspiring with somebody.

Humphrey In his interest.

Jim You know, Humphrey, honestly, I'm glad to be out of it. One makes too many compromises to hang on to a little power.

Humphrey Like going to the House of Lords, you mean?

Jim Yes. It's a paradox. Every time one goes up in the world one sinks a little lower.

Another shared moment of agreement.

Humphrey We're in the dustbin of history.

A sad silence.

Jim Excuse me a moment.

He stands as quickly as he can, and hurries into the hall.

Sophie You need help?

Jim (*exiting*) No.

Sophie He's sometimes caught short.

Humphrey I understand.

Sophie and Humphrey sit quietly.

Sophie I'm trying to learn how to work for him.

Humphrey You have my deepest sympathy.

Sophie He asked other people for their opinions? And listened?

Humphrey Yes. And no.

Sophie How did you make him listen to you?

Humphrey Bamboozlement. Or flattery.

She considers this.

Sophie Would you like a biscuit?

Humphrey He invited me for lunch, you know.

Sophie Sandwiches coming.

Humphrey Oh, very well.

He takes a biscuit.

Sophie Are most prime ministers good listeners?

Humphrey They're all different. Some are interesting thinkers, some are good leaders . . .

Sophie Which was he, a thinker or a leader?

Humphrey No.

Sophie (*amused*) I see.

Humphrey He meant well though.

Sophie I like him.

Humphrey Yes. Did his best.

Sophie What more can one ask?

Humphrey Plenty!

Jim (*off*) Sophie! Come here a minute, will you?

Sophie hurries out as we hear a loo flushing. Jim returns, helped by Sophie.

Um – tell me . . .

Humphrey You – er – your, um . . .

He gestures at Jim's trousers.

Jim What?

Humphrey Your – er – your fly is open.

Sophie goes to help him zip it up.

Jim Get off! I can do it.

She backs off, unoffended, and returns to the filing, listening.

Um – I was thinking about your tax scheme, how do you know you're actually going to live for another seven years?

Humphrey You don't, that's the gamble. The tax doesn't start reducing until after three years. It's been nearly three years so far, and frankly I'd rather die now than wait any longer. (*A grim smile.*) If I die they'll have to pay all the tax. Serve them right!

Jim But you'd rather live as long as you can, wouldn't you?

Humphrey I'm not sure any more. Don't think it'll be much longer.

Jim What makes you think you might die soon?

Humphrey I could choose to.

Jim (*shocked*) What, you mean, throw yourself under a train, or something?

Humphrey That's a bit melodramatic. You can just stop eating. That's all it takes, you know.

Jim Oh, I see. Hmm. That's good to know, actually.

Humphrey When the doctors at St Dymphna's assessed me they refused to keep me there. They demanded my son take me back. And when the pandemic hit I got out fast.

Jim I thought you wanted to die.

Humphrey I'm considering it, yes. I'm living now in a miserable, dark, slightly damp basement flat in the lovely big house in Islington they bought with *my* money. She's put me down for an old people's home. I'll have one pokey little room. This was not what was supposed to happen in my life. This was not what I was promised. I did everything right: a scholarship to Winchester, a scholarship to Oxford, a first in Classics, straight into the Civil Service as a high flyer, I looked correct, I spoke correctly, I wore the right tie. I was totally discreet. But look where I am now! Where are my seventy-two virgins, as it were?

Jim I can't help with that.

Humphrey Discarded. People of enormous ability –

Jim Like us –

Humphrey Like me, dispatched to a soulless institution, a place of bizarre antiseptic gentility like a funeral home, stuffed with geriatrics, not yet ready to die but thrown away. No matter what you've achieved you end up ignored, useless, forgotten.

Jim I'm not forgotten.

Humphrey I, who controlled the government and saved the country from going down the drain –

Jim Steady on. I wouldn't quite agree with that.

Humphrey (*gestures around*) But look at this. You landed on your feet. Here you are, Master of Hacker College, Oxford, without a care in the world. Living in the Master's Lodge, rent free. This is the life I should be living. Why am I not master of an Oxford college?

Jim Because I persuaded a billionaire to found the place and give it an endowment.

Humphrey You must admit it doesn't seem fair?

Jim I do admit that.

Humphrey In fact, I came here today because I need your help.

Jim (*ungracious*) Oh. That's not why I asked you here.

Humphrey Why did you?

Jim I need *your* help.

Humphrey You had my help for years.

Jim Sort of.

It's a stand-off.

All right then. What do you want?

Humphrey I need a job. So that I can afford a little place of my own where I can live out my life in comfort.

Jim What sort of job?

Humphrey Teaching. Visiting professor? Fellowship of some sort?

Jim You're a bit long in the tooth. The college doesn't give fellowships to anyone of your age.

Humphrey I'm not *any*one, I'm someone.

Jim Of course you are. But everyone else in the college retires at seventy-five at the latest.

Humphrey All right, not the college. A university faculty? – I could teach government, foreign affairs, diplomacy, anything . . .

Jim I could try, I suppose . . . but I could get Sophie a teaching post more easily than I could get you one.

Sophie (*interested*) Could you?

Jim You're young, you're Black, you're female, you're gay . . . you tick all the boxes. Write a play, the Royal Court will put it on.

Sophie I hadn't realised I was so fortunate. I'll remember that next time someone tells me to go back where I came from.

Humphrey Um – so – no chance you can help me?

Jim Humphrey, I'll do my best, for old times' sake. But first I need some help from you.

Humphrey Always a quid pro quo. What could you possibly need from me?

Jim I'm supposed to be the Master here in perpetuity. According to my contract they can't get rid of me. I negotiated a lifetime appointment for myself.

Humphrey In point of fact, I negotiated it for you.

Jim Did you? I didn't remember that.

Humphrey Of course you didn't.

Jim I've discovered my job is in jeopardy.

Humphrey What about a job for me? Can we do that first?

Jim My job situation is rather more of a priority than yours.

Humphrey Why is that?

Jim If *I* haven't got a job, I can't get you a job!

Humphrey How is your job in jeopardy?

Jim I've said a few things that were politically incorrect. It started when I was at a conference where I was due to make a speech, and I was in a lift. A young woman standing next to the buttons asked everyone, 'Which floor?' I said, 'Ladies lingerie, fifth floor.' It was just a joke. It turned out she was a Professor of Gender Studies somewhere and she made a formal complaint to the conference. I was 'no-platformed'. Couldn't deliver my speech.

Humphrey How utterly baffling.

Jim Yes. They want to throw me out of my job, and my home here, all because of a silly joke.

Humphrey What do you think, Sophie? Make any sense to you?

Sophie Yes. But they could be over-reacting.

Jim *Could* be?

Sophie Is that *all* you said?

Jim There's a few other silly little things. Nothing important but they were already against me.

Humphrey How I can help?

Jim You set this whole deal up for me.

Humphrey Oh, you remember that now?

Jim How could I forget?

Humphrey You did forget.

Jim Did I?

Humphrey Yes, I did set this up but that was then. I have no standing in this now.

Jim No one else can sort this out, you're my brain, at least you used to be, well occasionally anyway, so I need your help if your brain is still in full working order. (*Waits for a reply.*) Is it?

Humphrey It's slowed down a bit. I expect yours has too.

Jim You're sure?

Humphrey If you think I'm doolally, why are you asking for my help?

Jim There's no one else.

Humphrey Scraping the bottom of the barrel. (*Picks up his coat.*) I see.

Jim Oh sit down, Humphrey! Please. I didn't get to the top of the greasy pole by allowing people to roll over me.

Humphrey It would not be possible for people to roll over you at the top of a greasy pole.

Jim You sound just like Bernard.

Humphrey He was my protégé, I taught him to think like me.

Jim Yes, he never got over that. (*Sad.*) But I miss him.

Humphrey Me too.

Sophie (*after a moment*) Have some more coffee, Sir Humphrey. Nice and hot.

Humphrey What about lunch?

Sophie (*pouring more coffee*) I'll get the sandwiches in just a moment.

Humphrey hesitates, then sits near the door.

Jim Humphrey, this is a major crisis for me. I'm like you, I have no savings.

Humphrey Did you give it all to your daughter like I did?

Jim No, I'm not that stupid. But there wasn't anything to give. Not that she would have wanted anything from me, she was so rebellious and angry – do you remember that unless I did something to protect badgers she was going to stage a nude protest? Invite the press! Naked photos of a cabinet minister's daughter. To embarrass me.

Sophie She sounds like fun. I'd like to meet her.

Jim I bet you would. She's not a dyke though, if that's what you're thinking.

Sophie It wasn't. And I wish you wouldn't use that word.

Jim Sorry. I mean, she's not a lezzie.

Sophie shakes her head patiently.

What am I supposed it call it nowadays?

Sophie You'd be safe with LGBT.

Jim Fine. I don't think she's any of those.

Sophie I'd still like to meet her.

Jim I don't know where she is.

Humphrey How is it possible you have no savings to bequeath?

Jim Annie was ill for a long time. By the time she died I'd spent all my savings on her. There wasn't that much anyway, I'd never earned much as a political science lecturer at the LSE –

Humphrey I should hope not! Politics is not a science, it's an art. The art of the possible, as Bismarck said. Why are you laughing?

Sophie You not recognising political science as a discipline.

Humphrey Political science is an oxymoron. From the Greek 'oxys', meaning 'sharp' or 'keen', and 'moros', meaning 'foolish' – so, interestingly, and somewhat amusingly, the word 'oxymoron' – literal translation 'sharpfoolish' – is *itself* an oxymoron. A contradiction in terms within the word itself. Fascinating.

He chuckles. Jim stares at him.

Jim You find that amusing?

Humphrey I do.

Jim (*to Sophie*) You see what I had to put up with?

Humphrey Where are those sandwiches!

Sophie Right now! Sorry.

Sophie heads for the kitchen.

Jim Humphrey, what were we talking about?

Sophie (*calling back*) About how you didn't earn any money?

She's gone.

Jim Oh yes. I earned nothing significant as a journalist and editor of *Reform*. So there's just my pension from being PM.

Humphrey Isn't that pretty good?

Jim Not as good as the cabinet secretary's pension.

Humphrey What about your memoir? I thought I glimpsed it on the *Sunday Times* bestseller list. Oh look, a whole box, full of them!

He pulls two copies of Jim's book out of the box, one in each hand, and waves them at Jim.

Jim They wouldn't publish it that Christmas. Said no one would buy it. So it came out in May, a self-fulfilling prophecy. You only need to sell two thousand books to get on the hardback bestseller list in May.

Sophie (*returning with sandwiches*) Publishing's dying. Nobody would even publish my book. These are chicken, those are ham.

Humphrey takes a couple.

Jim You wrote a book?

Humphrey What was it called, dear lady?

Sophie *Femininity is Just a Male Social Construct.*

Humphrey (*dry*) And no one would publish it? How very surprising!

Jim My memoir reached number two on the *Sunday Times* list.

Humphrey Well *done*!

Jim But it was May! I sold about six thousand copies that week. That's all! You can hardly retire on the royalties from that. (*Ruminates.*) It was an awful book anyway.

Humphrey Oh yes, absolutely dreadful!

Jim (*defensive*) I didn't write it.

Humphrey Your name was all over it.

Jim I know. But the publisher didn't like what I wrote and brought in a ghost writer. From *The Sun*! I was lucky they didn't put in some page-three girls.

Sophie I would have liked that.

Humphrey Really?

Sophie grins.

Jim It was fairly humiliating to be pushed out of Number Ten but *really* humiliating to be fired from my own book.

Sophie That's awful, even if it was a rotten book.

Humphrey (*to Jim*) And no highly paid public appearances?

Jim All the others have cornered the market. But unlike most of my predecessors, my reputation is intact. I'm still somebody, a member of the House of Lords.

Sophie Ha!

Sophie is laughing. Humphrey too.

Jim What's so funny?

Humphrey Ozymandias?

Sophie Yes.

Jim What?

Sophie Ozymandias. It's by Shelley.

Jim Shelley who?

Sophie Percy Bysshe. You don't know it? It's a poem about the remnant of a huge ancient statue in the desert.

'And on the pedestal these words appear:
"My name is Ozymandias, King of Kings:
Look on my works, ye Mighty, and despair!"
Nothing beside remains. Round the decay
Of that colossal wreck, boundless and bare,
The lone and level sands stretch far away.'

Jim ponders this.

Jim I've never liked poetry really. Bit pointless. (*To Humphrey.*) I was surprised when you rejected the peerage I offered you.

Humphrey Why did *you* choose to go to the Lords? Not many ex-prime ministers do these days.

Jim I didn't want to lose all power.

Humphrey You didn't have much. The power wasn't real.

Jim It was. While it lasted.

Humphrey It wasn't. And it didn't. You made too many compromises to please your backbenchers.

Jim And to please the Civil Service.

Humphrey Nothing wrong with that. The Civil Service spoke for the country.

Jim Don't be ridiculous. You spoke for yourself and the Home Counties.

Humphrey Whereas you spoke for yourself and a few cronies who stuck with you because they had to.

Jim If my power was an illusion, so was yours.

Humphrey is forced to agree. He shrugs. They contemplate this.

Sophie Isn't all power an illusion? Ultimately?

Humphrey Yes, look at us now. We haven't even got power over where we live.

Jim I still have. At least I hope so, that's why you're here. (*Hasty.*) Not the only reason of course, it's good to see you. (*To Sophie.*) The world has changed in so many ways. Hard to understand.

Sophie It's not your fault. You were brought up with certain expectations, but we can see now that power is an outdated aggressive, male, patriarchal concept.

Humphrey We can see? Who the hell's 'we'? You mean you! That's *your* opinion.

Sophie Not just mine.

Humphrey Utter nonsense! Power is male, is it? – like Mrs Thatcher and Mrs Gandhi and Angela Merkel?

Sophie They weren't exactly feminine.

Jim You said 'femininity is just a male social construct'.

Sophie I think I've changed my mind since I wrote that book.

Jim Good thing nobody published it then.

Humphrey I hate it when people say 'we' when they mean 'I'.

Jim You used to do it all the time.

Humphrey That was different. I was speaking for the Civil Service.

Jim How could you know what they all thought?

Humphrey I made sure they were properly trained.

Sophie And thought what they were supposed to think? Isn't that a bit Orwellian?

Humphrey It's practical. It avoids the kind of chaos that's engulfed us now, with all those interfering spads they have today.

Sophie Spads?

Jim Special advisors.

Humphrey Short for 'spado'. You know what that means in Latin? Noun, third declension masculine. Means 'eunuch'. And that's what it still meant in my day. We shut them out! The machine ran smoothly.

Sophie To what end?

Humphrey Good government!

Sophie History doesn't exactly show that, does it? Look where we are now.

The phone rings.

Shall I get it?

Jim Yes. Please.

She answers the phone.

Sophie Hello? . . . Hi Jeff, is he on his way? . . .
Oh, the snow? . . .
I'll tell him.

She rings off.

Sir David's train can't get here because of the snow. The points are frozen. He hopes to come tomorrow.

Jim Oh God! Can you come back tomorrow?

Humphrey I doubt it. I'll ask Pavelcek. Who is Sir David?

Jim Sir David Knell is the college functionary who is trying to push me out.

Humphrey (*gets out his phone*) Oh, there's a text. He says if I want to get back tonight he has to come and get me now.

Jim Can he bring you back tomorrow?

Humphrey No. He's working tomorrow. If you want me here tomorrow, can I stay here overnight?

Jim Here??

Humphrey Well . . .

Sophie takes a decision.

Sophie Yes you can.

Jim (*startled*) What?

Sophie There's a spare bedroom upstairs. It's yours.

Humphrey I didn't bring anything with me. So I'd need to borrow a few things. A clean shirt tomorrow. Fresh underpants.

Jim (*horrified*) *My* underpants?

Sophie No problem. What else do you need?

Humphrey I always have my pills with me. What else? Oh, I'd need to borrow a toothbrush.

Jim You're very free with my underpants.

Sophie Yes. I'm the one who washes them.

Jim I don't want them back!

Sophie You want Sir Humphrey here, to talk to The Visitor?

Jim Yes.

Sophie Got a better idea?

Jim has no reply. Blackout.

Act Two

The next morning. It has stopped snowing but the landscape is white. Humphrey sits at the table eating breakfast; files have been moved to make room. Jim stares out of the window at the snow.

Jim I'm missing work today. A Lords debate, I said I'd go.

Sophie Is that work? Do they pay you?

Humphrey The Lords don't call it 'getting paid', dear lady, nothing so vulgar, they call it an attendance allowance. Three hundred and thirty two pounds per day.

Sophie Wow! How do you spend that much?

Jim We don't have to. It's not for expenses. All we have to do is clock in, then we can go straight home again. When Annie and I had a place in London I did that all the time. It was a lovely half-hour walk there and back.

Sophie You clock in, collect three hundred and thirty-two quid, clock out and go home? Sounds a bit sleazy, if you don't mind my –

Jim I do!

Humphrey (*egging her on*) Tax free. *Plus* expenses.

Jim That's how we're paid! Look, I'm sick of this, it's like bloody Prime Minister's Question Time here. Who do you think you are?

Sophie A taxpayer.

Jim I was prime minister of this ungrateful country and I was vilified after I left. They owe me, damn it! I have bills to pay. That's why we all go to work, right? Even if it's boring.

Sophie My job isn't boring. (*Starts clearing the table.*) Irritating, sometimes . . .

Humphrey But you have the prime minister's pension.

Jim Yes. Fifty-one thousand, seven hundred and thirty-five pounds. Not exactly a golden parachute.

Humphrey (*surprised*) Wasn't it index linked?

Jim Meaningless. Prime ministers' salaries didn't keep pace with inflation. And in those days, when you became prime minister, you were no longer eligible to keep the MP's pension and a minister's pension.

Humphrey Ah yes, I changed that in the Salaries and Pensions Act.

Jim After I resigned! Did you make it retrospective? No! Thanks a lot, Humphrey!

Humphrey I couldn't make it retrospective, you were so unpopular. And anyway legislation is seldom retrospective.

Jim So if I have to leave here, other than what I get for the Lords I'd have fifty-one thousand. Gross. Before tax. I can't live on that.

Sophie stops clearing the table.

Sophie You know what I live on?

Jim Look, all right, but I have to keep up appearances. And I don't even get the Lords attendance allowance very often any more, I can only get there when it really matters.

Sophie When would it matter?

Jim When I voted on Brexit, for instance.

Sophie Why would that have mattered? The Lords can't interfere with the will of the people.

Humphrey You really believe all that 'will of the people' stuff? Dear lady, if we listened to the will of the people we'd get hanging back. You don't want that, do you?

Sophie Oh. No.

Humphrey In my humble opinion it would be vastly preferable if the populace were to opine only if and when they exhibit and are able to both articulate and demonstrate sufficient proficiency, capability and epistemological dexterity to handle complex and perplexing diplomatic quandaries.

Sophie Um – can you put that another way?

Jim He means it might be better if the people knew what they were talking about before they spoke.

Sophie Do the politicians?

Humphrey Of course not. Politicians often speak from a position of total ignorance. Maybe it's appropriate for the public to do the same. (*Mischievous.*) In fact, I would argue that if the voters knew what they were talking about, it might create a dangerous precedent.

Jim Very droll, Humphrey.

Humphrey I'm serious. Why did we have that damn referendum? For centuries our government has been a parliamentary democracy. That means people voted for representatives who decided things for them. Ordinary people didn't presume to make important decisions about policy, certainly not about changing the constitution. It was none of their damn business! They didn't know enough and they knew they didn't know. Once a government was in power, it would say, 'We have a mandate,' and then go ahead and change the constitution if they felt like it, like they did with the Lords reform and devolution.

Jim I agree that most people had absolutely no grasp of what Brexit would involve, but the will of the people was expressed in that vote and could not be ignored.

Sophie (*increduous*) You're saying that the people knew what was best for them even though they didn't know anything about it?

Humphrey That's the fiction on which democracy is based: The people know what's best for them *even when* they don't know what they're talking about. Which is most of the time, obviously.

Jim My problem was the hard Brexit versus the soft Brexit.

Sophie That's so Freudian. Soft brexit: limp. Hard brexit: erect! All those politicians competing to prove they have the biggest dicks.

Jim Ha! No problem for me there.

Humphrey It might be more elegant to say that the problem was that Brexit was like boiling an egg: while they were endlessly discussing whether it would be better hard or soft, it went rotten.

Sophie Something was rotten in the state of Brexit.

Humphrey Yes, the Leavers said the referendum wouldn't be binding – and when they won, it suddenly became binding after all.

Jim You must admit they handled that rather well.

Sophie It would have been better if they told the truth.

Jim Truth changes. Truth is pliable, truth is elusive, truth is a matter of interpretation and opinion.

Humphrey You want truth? Get rid of the politicians.

Sophie Which ones?

Humphrey All of them. All the squalid vote-grubbers who'll do anything for the sake of party unity – as if anything could matter less. Get thee gone, the lot of you!

Jim Don't be absurd. Who would run the country?

Sophie (*interested*) You don't really believe in democracy, do you, Sir Humphrey?

Humphrey Moderation in all things.

Sophie How does democracy work in moderation?

Humphrey Democracy would be good for the Russians, Syrians, Iraqis, Iranians, Saudis, Chinese . . .

Sophie Overseas people, in fact.

Humphrey As it happens. Democracy is the collision of legitimate vested interests. The moderation that's needed is respect for those who disagree with you.

Jim He's right.

Sophie You're actually *agreeing* with each other?

Humphrey Not entirely. It may seem a revolutionary concept, but I think people who are *qualified* should run the country?

Jim He means him.

Humphrey Or someone like me.

Jim That *would* be a precedent.

Humphrey Not at all. I ran your government.

Jim I ran it!

Humphrey No, with respect, all you did was appease your party.

Getting annoyed with each other.

Jim They were right to send you to St Dymphna's. I think you belong in a locked ward.

Humphrey Then why did you phone me if you thought I was deranged? As soon as I retired, your government started to fall apart.

Jim You never used to be so confrontational.

Humphrey I was obliged to appear deferential when I was with you. My job. But when I reached my seventy-fifth birthday I decided I had earned the right to say what I think, to everybody, whether it caused offence or not. (*Thinks.*) It was soon after that my daughter-in-law put me away in St Dymphna's.

Jim That would explain it.

Sophie Let's all calm down.

There's a silence.

Jim Maybe things will change for the better. We did need to gain control of our borders and our own currency.

Sophie I thought we already had that.

Humphrey We did.

Sophie What was wrong with freedom of movement?

Humphrey Nothing. It was all about fear of Muslims and terrorists.

Sophie Fear of Muslims? What about all the violent Christians? You saying immigrants caused the rise in street crime?

Jim No, that happened because a thousand police stations were closed. Twenty per cent fewer bobbies on the beat. A stupid decision by the Home Office. The Home Office is a law unto itself and completely idiotic!

Humphrey The Home Office believes that immigrants take jobs from the Brits.

Sophie Brits don't want my job.

Jim She's right. I couldn't find anyone else.

Sophie Oh, thanks a lot! You want to know what I believe?

Jim Um – okay, if you want to tell us.

Sophie I believe most people want to show kindness and humanity towards each other.

Jim I can tell you've never been in the Cabinet. Humphrey, why were you so keen on austerity?

Humphrey (*thoughtful*) Good question.

The problem is, in economics, the questions keep changing. So the answers change as well. The odd thing is, even if the questions don't change, the answers do.

Jim That's exactly why no one ever knows what to do in an economic crisis. It's always new.

Humphrey I'm afraid I now resemble an economist. I used to think I knew the answers, but now I don't even know the questions.

Sophie Wasn't austerity because you were frightened of inflation?

Humphrey Yes. I was hypnotised by the deficit. I was a deer caught in the headlights.

Jim I was because you were. My relationship with you was like a rabbit with a snake.

Humphrey Which were you?

Jim You were the snake.

Humphrey That's the first time I've ever heard a prime minister refer to himself as a rabbit.

The phone rings. Sophie gets it.

Sophie Yes? (*Rings off.*) It's Sir David. He's coming over from the Porter's Lodge.

Jim When?

Sophie Now.

They all look at each other.

Jim Oh God. I didn't expect him so soon.

Sophie Do you need to go to the loo before he comes?

Jim (*embarrassed*) No! Look, Humphrey. If the college meeting was held yesterday, they've just briefed him. This could be ugly.

Humphrey Surely this can't all be about the lingerie. I'm trying to recall . . . Didn't I see something in the papers about you and what's-his-name? – Cecil Rhodes.

Jim A storm in a teacup. I was at a private dinner party with the Master of Oriel College and someone asked if *I* thought that statue of Cecil Rhodes should have been removed. I said on the whole I thought not.

Sophie Not?

Jim You think it should have been removed?

Sophie Of course it should!

Jim My point is, somebody recorded me secretly, and showed it online.

Sophie Why do all you politicians keep forgetting there's no privacy any more?

Humphrey I am emphatically not a politician.

Jim What am I supposed to do? Never have a frank conversation, even in private? Nothing would ever get done. Not that that would bother you, Humphrey, you devoted your entire career to the cause of nothing getting done.

Humphrey I certainly did devote much of my career to fighting foolish unthought-out changes being made by foolish thoughtless people.

Jim Elected people.

Humphrey The world's in chaos, one disastrous decision after another is being made across the globe by ideological and theocratic strongmen –

Jim It's the swing of the pendulum. Sometimes things have to get worse before they get better.

Humphrey So it's all right to put people in mental hospitals because they disagree with you?

Jim You mean, like the Russians do?

Humphrey Not like the Russians, like my daughter-in-law!

Jim What were we talking about?

Humphrey I've no idea. (*Blows his nose.*) Excuse me.

Sophie The Cecil Rhodes statue at Oriel College.

Humphrey That's right. I find it hard to believe they'd make you resign just because you said that statue should stay.

Sophie (*she knows more*) It's not just because of that. Is it?

The front door bell rings.

Shall I let him in?

Jim Yes.

Sophie exits.

Remember, I can't help you unless you help me.

Humphrey I know. Like the old days. United we stand.

Sophie re-enters with Sir David.

Jim (*jovial*) Good morning. Back again?

David Morning, Lord Hacker. (*Sees Humphrey and Sophie.*) May we have a private discussion?

Jim That's ironic, don't you think? You're here because I was secretly recorded – privacy doesn't exist any more. This is Sir Humphrey Appleby, retired cabinet secretary.

David Delighted to meet you.

They shake hands.

Jim He's my legal advisor.

Humphrey Um, not exactly, I'm not a lawyer.

Jim And this is Sophie . . . um, Sophie Something, she's my student politics advisor.

Sophie (*surprised*) Am I?

Jim Let's all sit down.

They all sit.

David The junior common room – the undergraduates – and the middle common room – graduate students – and the Fellows had their meetings this morning. By a significant majority they asked for your resignation.

Jim When?

David This morning.

Jim I know when the meeting was. When do they want me to resign?

David This morning.

Jim This morning?

David We're happy to attribute it to ill-health.

Jim (*stands up abruptly*) There's nothing wrong with my health. Ow! I may resign one day but that's entirely up to me. Isn't that right, Humphrey?

Humphrey says nothing.

Speak up, Humphrey!

Humphrey Yes, you see, this was indeed a lifetime appointment, which I negotiated. Don't you think this is all an absurd over-reaction to a silly joke about 'women's lingerie, fifth floor' and an even sillier comment about the Cecil Rhodes statue?

Jim It wasn't silly – you may disagree but it wasn't silly.

David Sir Humphrey, I'm afraid you don't know the whole picture. Lord Hacker said a few other things at that dinner.

Jim In a *private* conversation.

David Admittedly. But you said that the empire did a huge amount of good. You said it taught Africans Christianity and civilisation.

Sophie Did you really say that?

Jim I was slightly drunk.

Sophie You forgot about the slave trade? Or was that part of the civilising process?

David It was all recorded and put out on TikTok.

Sophie Of course.

David And you said that in India the British did much more good than harm, gave the natives trains and made them run on time.

Jim That's what Churchill thought.

Sophie (*genuinely curious*) You were able to ignore the fact that you destroyed a couple of thousand years of Indian culture, exploited the people, made them poor and the British rich?

Jim I had nothing to do with that. That was a hundred and fifty years ago.

David But you didn't condemn it.

Jim I wasn't giving a balanced view, I was just chatting.

David Saying the empire was good for India. Is that what you think?

Humphrey Of course he doesn't.

David Lord Hacker?

Jim I don't know. Depends who I'm talking to. But – what if I do? Whatever happened to free speech?

Humphrey Indeed. This is a university, where ideas should be freely expressed and exchanged.

David Yes. The college welcomes open debate and freedom of expression –

Jim Bollocks! The college welcomes it in *theory* but in practice you want it stamped out as quickly as possible and you'll blacklist or sack anybody who has an opinion different from a vocal minority.

David The majority, in this instance. But Lord Hacker, no one is obstructing your free speech. You can say anything you like as an individual but not when you represent the college.

Humphrey He wasn't representing the college, he was at a private dinner party.

David So long as he's Master he always represents the college. Like the monarch.

Jim They don't know what I think.

Humphrey They do now!

Jim Humphrey, you're supposed to be on my side.

Humphrey I'm hoping that, in your interest and the interests of the college, we can all get on to the same side.

David I'm afraid it's a bit late for that. Lord Hacker, let me put it in a way you might understand. You were an MP. The college is your constituency. We are de-selecting you because you don't represent your constituents any more.

Humphrey Is there no compromise possible?

David If he made an apology, perhaps?

Jim I won't apologise. Why should I? It's just history.

David History's important.

Jim You can't apply modern standards to historical events.

Humphrey Supposing Lord Hacker agreed to make no public statements until they have been checked by the Fellows.

David All public statements would have to be authorised in advance to make sure they were in compliance with the college's zero tolerance and safe space policies.

Jim But these weren't public statements.

David All statements, then.

Jim Everything I say, to anyone, anywhere?

David Yes.

Jim Don't be daft.

David In case you're being recorded.

Jim Fuck off.

Humphrey I'm not *sure* you're helping your case.

David There's your answer, Sir Humphrey: that compromise is not practical, partly because his Lordship's views on imperialism are far from the only problem.

Humphrey Oh God! What else is there?

David There is a feeling, sir, among the students and the Fellows too, that you are out of touch.

Jim A 'feeling'?

David Yes.

Jim Out of touch?

David Yes.

Jim How can I be out of touch? I listen to the *Today* programme and the *World at One* and *PM* and the *Ten O'Clock News*. And even *Newsnight*, God help me.

David Perhaps I should have said 'reactionary'.

Jim (*incredulous*) Reactionary?

Humphrey You're repeating everything he says.

Jim I'm repeating everything he says?

Humphrey You're repeating everything he says.

Humphrey and Sophie nod.

Jim It's because I can't believe my ears!

David Instead of being supportive in the students' quest for safe spaces and trigger warnings, you have been openly oppositional. You are not sensitive to the students' feelings.

Humphrey Perhaps they're not sensitive to his.

David Should they be?

Jim They bloody should! Respect! They're students! I was prime minister! This is all because a few undergraduates in American Studies boycotted a tutorial because when they were reading some book called *The Fire Next Time* by James Spalding –

Sophie Baldwin.

Jim Balding?

Sophie Bald*win*.

Jim They were angry because they weren't given a trigger warning to warn them the book uses what they called an offensive word. Preposterous nonsense!

Humphrey What was the word?

Jim 'Negro.'

There is an awkward silence. They all turn and look at Sophie. She says nothing.

Humphrey Just to clarify – 'Negro'? Not the n-word?

David 'Negro' is an n-word.

Humphrey Not *the* n-word.

Jim Apparently 'Negro' also offends people now. Is that right, Sophie?

Sophie Yep.

Jim But wasn't it the word everyone used when he wrote the book?

Sophie When he wrote it? Yes, back then, in the sixties.

Jim The defence rests. Balding was Black and he used the word 'Negro'. Why the hell shouldn't the lecturer?

David The lecturer is a white male in 2023. It hurt the feelings of a couple of our more sensitive students who regard themselves as victims of racism.

Jim Sophie?

Sophie I don't want to get into this.

Jim So what should we do? Censor the book? Expurgate it? Ban it?

David Well, no, not . . .

Jim Good God, we fought these censorship battles years ago. Remember the *Lady Chatterley's Lover* case, Humphrey? I remember reading it in the fourth form, behind the bike sheds. It was great! Sorry, Sophie, but they use all sorts of naughty words like . . .

Humphrey (*interrupts*) I think what Lord Hacker's trying to say . . . is that the end of censorship was a significant step towards freedom.

Jim Right, we wouldn't use those words in polite company but they're an integral part of what Florence wrote.

Humphrey D. H. Florence?

Jim Yes. Words are just . . . words. 'Sticks and stones may break my bones but words –'

Sophie May I ask a question?

David Please do.

Sophie Would it be okay with you to use words like wogs and wops and chinks, and call Jews Shylocks and Jew-boys, and gays pooftahs? In class?

Jim No. But, if those words are used in a book which is important enough to be on the syllabus, then – yes, it's all right, necessary even, to quote them in that context.

Humphrey It's just a *word* that's at issue! There's nothing intrinsically offensive about a word.

Sophie Not even the d-word?

Humphrey What's that?

Sophie Deranged. You said it was offensive.

Humphrey That's different.

Sophie Oh. So it's okay to use words that are offensive to minorities and gays because they're just words – but it's not okay to use words that are offensive to you.

Humphrey I would never call someone a wop to his face, which incidentally is an acronym for Without Papers.

Sophie Why wouldn't you?

Humphrey In case it caused offence.

Sophie Exactly!!

Jim Thank you, Sophie, you've said quite enough, we didn't ask for your opinion.

Sophie You did, actually.

Jim You're just clouding the argument. Pipe down.

Humphrey (*becoming emotional*) And while we're on the subject, why would I want to cause offence to pooftahs? I went to a boys' boarding school, I grew up with them, some of my best friends – I was an altarboy, for God's sake, I was educated by pooftah priests. If we can't even utter the words the author uses, how can the book be discussed?

Sophie says nothing.

Jim Go on. Answer him.

Sophie I was piping down.

Jim He asked you, how can the book be discussed if you can't say key words that are in it?

Sophie Maybe it shouldn't be.

Jim Shouldn't be discussed? But if it's on the syllabus . . .

Humphrey You think James Baldwin's use of the word 'Negro' is a reason not to read *The Fire Next Time* even though it's a work by a very important Black writer?

Sophie Students of colour should be warned, in case they want to choose not to read the book.

David Precisely. A trigger warning.

Humphrey Would you want a trigger warning?

Sophie I'm not getting into this.

Jim They shouldn't be able to choose, dammit! They should read it if it's on the bloody syllabus.

Sophie Why? Who says?

Jim Because they come here to be educated.

Sophie What does education mean? Being told what to think?

Jim No. It means opening the mind to new ideas.

Sophie That would be good. You know there's a demand for the inclusion of African literature and queer literature?

Jim That's just silly!

Sophie What's silly about it?

Jim We can't teach everything.

Sophie So no new ideas after all!

Jim Be reasonable. We can't push out the Western canon.

Sophie It's still there for those who want to study it. I did. Words may just be words . . . but words can hurt. The students want to feel safe.

Jim They don't want freedom of speech, they want freedom *from* speech.

Humphrey (*reminiscing*) How well I remember visiting America in the early sixties. It was a linguistic minefield. In those days, Sophie, we *had* to use the word 'Negro'. Or 'coloured'. That was the choice. You couldn't say 'Black'. 'Black' was considered an insult. Then, paradoxically, it *all* changed when Black Power came in. Until then I didn't even dare ask for a cup of black coffee in case it caused offence to a Neg— Black waitress. You had to say 'coffee without cream'. Now we can't say 'coloured people' but we're supposed to say 'people of colour'. Why is that?

Sophie All you're saying is that conventions change. They do, but they still matter, you know that. People have the right to self-identify.

Jim Um – I know there are strong feelings but how about we all calm down and have a nice cup of tea?

Sophie The answer to everything, right?

Jim Yes, it's our national drink.

Sophie Tea comes from India, it's a colonialist drink.

Jim (*explodes*) Sophie, for God's sake, shut up with all this woke nonsense.

Sophie That was a joke.

David (*chuckling*) I thought it was funny.

Jim Go and make the tea.

Sophie Is that still my purview? I thought I was recently appointed your student politics advisor.

She heads for the kitchen.

Jim You're also my carer.

She freezes, mid-stage, but does not turn back.

Care worker.

She exits. Humphrey wanders around.

Humphrey I'm looking for my briefcase. (*To David.*) I did some homework on this Cecil Rhodes thing, because I'd read in *The Times* what Jim – er Lord Hacker – was quoted as saying. (*Finds it, extracts papers.*) Where are my glasses? Oh, here. Do you know that student activists persuaded Liverpool University to remove Gladstone's name from a hall of residence because his money came from his father who made it from slavery?

Jim That's not his fault!

David I hold no brief for Liverpool. But the students said Gladstone used the money and was insufficiently vocal in condemning the slavery that made his family rich.

Humphrey Protesters are defacing Churchill's statue again too.

Jim Gladstone and Churchill! Our two greatest prime ministers, if you don't count me. This trigger-warning stuff, it's all gone too far.

Humphrey Where will it end, I wonder?

Jim Not here. I read, in *Cherwell*, that some students here are refusing to express an opinion in tutorials in case it offends anyone.

Humphrey Seriously?

Jim They don't want to appear insensitive or aggressive or something worse. It's this bloody concept of the vulnerable student. Why should we take it for granted that students are mentally fragile? They should toughen up!

Humphrey Sir, are you in fact saying that any contrary opinion about the empire or the Middle East will be construed as racism?

David I'm saying nothing, I'm merely the messenger, communicating the college's request for Lord Hacker's immediate resignation.

Humphrey If he does resign –

Jim He won't! And you know why? The college needs money. We are becoming too dependent on international students because they pay us three times as much. Hacker College is only thirteen years old and finances are on a knife edge with no wealthy alumni yet.

David That's true, but –

Jim The only donations we get are from corporations and wealthy individuals. They've dried up. And who got them for us? I did. I already told the Fellows I can extract a huge new donation from the very generous but discreet chap who endowed the millions that built this place.

David I'm afraid that only fanned the flames.

Humphrey Why?

David He's a Russian oligarch.

Jim Oh yes.

Humphrey Did he make any conditions for the new donation?

Jim Only one.

David What?

Jim I promised to put up a statue of him.

David He's a gangster! His funds are known to be the proceeds of organised crime.

Jim They knew that when the college took his money in the first place! Besides, we could have the money laundered.

Humphrey and David clap their hands over their ears.

Humphrey I didn't hear you say that.

David Nor did I.

Jim I said –

Humphrey *and* **David** We heard!

Jim I want to know who led this movement against me.

David That's not relevant.

Jim It is to me. People aren't perfect. Even the greatest of us sometimes make mistakes, yes, even me. You have to judge great men by the totality of their lives and their achievements. If we can only have statues of people who are perfect, that just leaves Jesus Christ.

Sophie returns with a tray of cups of tea as David shakes his head and stands. He places a letter and an envelope on a table.

David I have to go. I shall leave this letter with you to sign. You or somebody can drop it into the Porter's Lodge.

Humphrey And if he refuses?

David I wouldn't advise it.

Humphrey And if I wish to talk to you further . . .

David I shall be lunching in hall. Good day.

David leaves. There is a sombre silence. Sophie puts down the tea tray.

Jim Why have they no loyalty to me?

Humphrey I'm sure they feel loyal to the college.

Jim She doesn't.

Sophie No I don't.

Humphrey How extraordinary!

Sophie Yes, isn't it odd? When I was a student here I loved being viewed as a cashpoint and I was *thrilled* to watch my debt grow bigger and bigger. Did you ever see an old TV series called *The Invisible Man*? He had to wear bandages –

Jim (*overlapping*) Ah yes, bandages!

Sophie And sunglasses –

Jim Sunglasses!

Humphrey Black hat.

Sophie – and sunglasses and gloves, otherwise he couldn't be seen. I was the Invisible Woman. I needed the bandages.

Jim I get it. You were caught in a web of privilege and totally excluded?

Humphrey It's not possible to be excluded from a web you are caught in.

Jim Thank you, Humphrey, for that clarification.

Sophie No one knew what I was doing here. After a while, nor did I. I'd wake up late in the day, and spend the rest of it in a haze of weed and takeaways. But nobody noticed. Eventually I asked for help and it took eight weeks before I was offered regular counselling.

Humphrey Did you manage to scrape some sort of degree?

Sophie A first, like you.

Humphrey Goodness me! How extraordinary!

Sophie Black women can get firsts too.

Humphrey I didn't mean that –

Sophie I worked hard and put all the shit out of my mind. But I didn't forget it and I still owe thousands of pounds. At nine per cent interest. Why should I be grateful? Or loyal? I clean up, make the bed, clean the toilet, help you get dressed, wash your underpants . . .

Jim This is your choice. Get a better job.

Sophie I will, eventually. But everybody needs to be needed.

Jim You're saying you need me?

Sophie No. You need me.

Jim (*stunned*) I could find somebody else.

Sophie Really?

Jim Maybe.

Sophie I do this because I'm very sorry for you and I want to help.

Jim You don't need to be sorry for me!

Humphrey Nor me!

Sophie Oh shut up, both of you. You and your fragile old egos. I'm happy to help you, I'm just tired of not being *seen*!

Humphrey When I was in Whitehall I found there was a considerable advantage in not being seen.

Jim Yes, so when you screwed up it looked like my fault.

Sophie You don't really see me. But I see you. Your loss. You both had so much and you blew it. I can't just walk out on you.

Jim Ridiculous!

Sophie Who else is there? Who's left? Your family? Your cabinet? The party? Did you have any real friends?

Jim No, I was in politics.

Sophie You had a driver? Where's he?

Jim I don't know.

Sophie You don't even exchange Christmas cards? What about your daughter?

Jim shrugs hopelessly.

Nobody's interested any more. Only the media, and only when you say something politically incorrect.

Jim And when I die. They'll have the obits ready.

Sophie What do you want them to say?

Jim 'He was much greater than he was given credit for.'

Humphrey You'll be lucky!

Sophie But I'm happy to stay and help if I'm being heard.

Jim Good. I hear you, now can you get us some more tea?

Sophie That's all you want me for, to pop in and out with cups of tea?

Jim This is cold!

Sophie Get it yourself. It'd be good for you.

She sits down.

Jim Humphrey, what can I do about this?

Humphrey About getting more tea?

Jim About being evicted!

Humphrey There may be certain avenues still to be explored. In point of fact, as far as one can see, looking at it by and large, as it were, within the college guidelines and statutes perhaps we could adopt a more flexible posture – draft a more persuasive case, mobilise support with a little give and take if we try taking a view bearing in mind both sides with a recognition by all parties that what is happening is not quite cricket, maybe there are other possibilities not yet fully explored . . . after all, there hasn't been an inquiry, at least not one at which you have had the opportunity to express your point of view, or not necessarily, or not in an appropriate forum, even though you may have already expressed your viewpoint only too clearly on numerous other occasions, so in general terms . . . so, at the end of the day, not to put too fine a point on it . . . (*He stops.*) I'm sorry, Prime Minister, I can't quite remember what I was trying to say.

Jim Where did you think you were going with it?

Humphrey I don't know. (*Puts his head in his hands.*) Nowhere.

Sophie (*gently*) How would you like a drink? A real drink.

Humphrey Oh yes! Scotch please. How did you know?

Sophie I'm a care worker. (*At the drinks table.*) Anything in it?

Humphrey A little water.

Sophie pours and brings it to him.

Sophie How about you?

Jim The same. Please.

She goes to get another.

Humphrey Perhaps I should pop over to hall and have one more quick word with The Visitor before he finishes lunch?

Jim Without me?

Humphrey Yes.

Jim Why?

Humphrey I think I might be more persuasive without you.

Sophie Do you really think there'd be any point?

Humphrey Not really. No.

Humphrey sips his Scotch.

Jim I know! I have an idea! Why don't we leak it to the press that they're pushing me out?

Humphrey I'm not sure they'd sympathise.

Sophie The *Guardian* wouldn't. You might get the *Mail* on your side, but that would be counterproductive in the college. In fact, it would probably be the final nail in your coffin.

Jim I used to understand how things worked.

Humphrey There are no guy ropes any more.

Jim None.

Humphrey Look at cricket. It used to be a leisurely, quiet, calm game. Everyone behaved honourably. If you knew you were out, you didn't wait for the umpire to say so, you just did the gentlemanly thing and walked from the crease. Now . . . most of the time they don't even play in white!

Sophie The end of civilisation as we know it!

Jim Never mind cricket. The world has changed.

Humphrey The British have changed.

Sophie Yes, we have.

Jim And what can *we* do, Humphrey? Nothing. We're invisible now.

Humphrey When we were in charge, things worked. (*Before Sophie interrupts.*) Not for everyone. Not everywhere – but mostly. It's goodbye to all that. Put out to grass.

Jim When I voted in the Lords it was obvious we should *remain* in Europe . . . but I voted for Brexit like everyone else. Now the lights are going out all over Europe. Or, maybe, all over Britain. Not sure. The big problem is, there's no one of my intellectual calibre in charge here any more.

Humphrey Yes, at least we must count our blessings.

They smile at each other. All animosity has gone.

Jim Everything changed for me when Annie died.

Sophie How do you feel about not having a relationship with Lucy?

Jim With Annie gone, Lucy's gone too. (*Weeps.*) I could have been a better father, I know.

Humphrey I expected too much of my son. He gave up ancient Greek in the fourth form. Then he only had Latin but he couldn't even translate a passage from Caesar's *Gallic Wars*. I thought, he must have some aptitude for something. But no. Just carpentry.

Sophie That's not so bad. Jesus was a carpenter.

Humphrey Or, depending which gospel you read, a descendent of King David. They're all fiction anyway.

Sophie What's wrong with being a carpenter?

Humphrey It's just not what I hoped.

Sophie Does he build things?

Humphrey Yes. Furniture and stuff.

Sophie What did *you* build?

Humphrey has no reply.

It's his life, not yours.

Humphrey I know. Yes. I suppose so.

Sophie Do you think you were a bit condescending, maybe?

Humphrey Certainly not.

Jim Of course you were.

Humphrey How would you know?

Jim You always are.

Humphrey (*ponders*) Perhaps I should stop calling his wife the Evil Queen.

Jim (*amused*) You call her that to her face?

Humphrey No, but I think she overheard me once or twice when I wasn't thinking.

Sophie Maybe you should stop thinking of her like that.

Humphrey Yes. Perhaps it's not all her fault. Bit late now, though.

Jim Hey, I have another idea! I could accuse the college of elder abuse.

Sophie and Humphrey look at him and then each other in disbelief.

How about if I got a private detective to find some dirt on one of the ringleaders?

Humphrey Dirt isn't what it used to be.

Jim It can be. Any accusation of inappropriate sexual behaviour can get you thrown out of college.

Sophie Sexting too.

Humphrey Sexting? You mean, texting photographs?

Sophie Yes. Selfies.

Jim Of their private parts? Great!

Sophie I had a friend that did it once or twice. She had a very busy sex life. I thought it was stupid. And dangerous. I'd rather send a selfie of my brain but that technology doesn't exist yet.

Jim Sophie, you know what? Much to my surprise, I find I'm becoming increasingly fond of you.

Sophie Even when I pipe up?

Jim But you can't care for me for long, much as I like you. I respect you too much. You must find something better to do.

Sophie crosses to him and kisses him gently on the top of his head.

Sophie I will when I'm ready.

Jim, touched, wipes his eyes again.

Jim Wait! Here's another idea: What if one of the ringleaders of the Fellows is forging cheques and screwing an undergraduate . . .?

Sophie Simultaneously? Forging cheques and shagging? Multitasking?

Humphrey Have you any evidence of that?

Jim No, I just made it up, but it could be true, maybe Sophie could start the rumour on social media.

Humphrey If it were traced to you you'd have a libel action on your hands. And you wouldn't get legal aid, not since all the cuts you made in the Justice department.

Sophie Aren't you both forgetting something?

Jim *and* **Humphrey** What?

Sophie It wouldn't be honest.

Jim *and* **Humphrey** Oh. Yes. Hmm. S'pose not. Interesting.

Jim I'm trying not to panic. Where will I live if I'm forced out of the Master's Lodge?

Humphrey I expect you'll find somewhere.

Jim They can't force me out. Can they?

Humphrey It looks as though they can. And will.

Jim Have they no respect? (*Deep sadness.*) I'll probably die holding the hand of a total stranger.

Sophie Like most people. The world relies on strangers who rely on strangers.

Humphrey When I saw my doctor five years ago he thought I might have some sort of liver disease. (*Finishes his whisky.*) I asked him what the prognosis is. He said: 'Oh, don't worry, how old are you?'

I told him.

'No problem,' he said. 'We only have to keep you going for about another five years.' I was shocked.

I said, 'Five? How about another ten or fifteen?' He apologised and said he just meant statistically. Maybe so – but why would he say it?

Jim I know what you mean. If I were to die tomorrow people would ask my age and say, 'Oh well, he had a good innings.' But that's not how it looks to me. I'm not ready to go yet.

Humphrey nods. They contemplate this sad truth.

Sophie, I'll be without a home if I have to leave here.

Sophie With your prime minister's pension, plus the Lords tax-free expenses, you won't be sleeping under Charing Cross Bridge.

Jim Humphrey, might they give me a room in college? Can you get that for me?

Humphrey If they're pushing you out they won't want you around. Maybe they'd make a contribution to a cottage somewhere else. The Outer Hebrides?

Jim Such ingratitude.

Humphrey Gratitude is merely a lively expectation of favours to come. You have nothing to give them any more, except problems.

Jim They have jobs here because of me.

Humphrey But they have them, that's the point. You don't have the power to take them away.

Jim So . . . what do you suggest, Sophie?

Sophie Pray?

Jim Did you say pray?

Humphrey Do you believe in God? Is that a conventional woke view?

Sophie I'm not conventionally woke.

Humphrey I know it's customary for people of our age to turn to God. I've had thoroughly religious friends tell me out of the blue, 'I'm ready to meet my maker.' But I've come to the conclusion that I'm not, comforting though the thought might be. I'm increasingly sceptical about God.

Jim Me too. I have a question: if there *is* a God, why does he run the world like the Home Office?

Humphrey Are you confident in your belief?

Sophie No – but, as experience has told Black people we can't have faith in Man, I try to have faith in God.

Humphrey Do you succeed?

Sophie Not quite. But there are more things in heaven and earth, Horatio, than are dreamt of in your philosophy.

Jim He's not Horatio, he's Humph— Oh, I see, sorry. Wait a minute . . . I've just had an idea!

They groan quietly.

No, listen. You gave your savings and assets to your son and his wife to avoid death duties, but what about your pension? I know mine can't be assigned to anyone. I bet yours can't be either.

Humphrey They've been giving me an allowance, I never questioned it . . . Perhaps they stole my pension too, and used it . . . How absolutely extraordinary!

Jim That they did that?

Humphrey No, that you thought of this and I didn't.

Jim (*offended*) I don't think that's so extraordinary.

Sophie If you didn't give up your pension, you're no more destitute that he is. You could rent yourself a little place too. Here in Oxford.

Jim Humphrey, must I accept defeat?

Humphrey Looks like it.

Sadness envelops them.

Sophie If you can't change something, try to change the way you think about it.

Jim Bumper-sticker bullshit. There is nothing good about aging.

Sophie You acquire wisdom, maybe?

Jim What's the point of that? You don't get wisdom until it's too late to be much use to you.

Sophie You phoned Sir Humphrey perhaps because you wanted him to solve your problem. You must have realised he can't. (*To Humphrey.*) You came because you wanted Lord Hacker to help you get a teaching job – but obviously that would be impossible at your age, an occasional lecture maybe, but a full-time job? No way. So why did you really call him? Why did you really come?

Humphrey You tell me.

Sophie Perhaps you need friendship. Maybe you've always needed him.

Jim That's silly. We've never been friends.

Humphrey Just colleagues.

Sophie You're reaping the reward of a life poorly spent.

Jim I was prime minister!

Sophie I'm talking personally.

Humphrey Um – why are you saying all this to him?

Sophie I'm saying it to you too.

Humphrey How dare you!

Sophie Why don't you pool your resources and move in together?

Humphrey Quarantined with him forever? Christ! What a thought!

Sophie You might annoy each other but you wouldn't be lonely. It's good to have company. I'd come in and take care of you both, when I could. (*She waits.*) 'Thank you' might be the phrase you're looking for.

Jim Why should I thank you? I'd have to share you with him.

Sophie I'll take that as a sort of compliment.

Jim Without Annie, I don't know what to think any more. I feel completely lost. And without you, actually, Humphrey. In a funny way, we did have – you know – a friendship, really.

Humphrey In an odd way, yes.

Jim You feel the same?

Humphrey (*cautious*) Yes . . . maybe we could give it a go.

Jim Together again at last. How awful!

Then they smile at each other.

Humphrey Yes, Prime Minister.

Lights slowly fade to black.